ECHOES FROM
NIGERIA

Echoes from Nigeria

ECHOES FROM
NIGERIA

A collection of poems

Nwodibo Ekechukwu

**WORDS
RHYMES &
RHYTHM**

For information about permission to reproduce
selections from this book, write to *info@wrr.ng* or
nwasonde@yahoo.com.

National Library of Nigeria Cataloguing-in-Publication
Data

Cover Design: Akila Jibrin

Printed and Published in Nigeria by:
Words Rhymes & Rhythm Limited
Suite C309, Global Plaza Plot 366, Obafemi Awolowo
Way, Jabi District, Abuja, Nigeria.
08169027757, 08060109295
www.wrr.ng

DEDICATION

This book is dedicated to my dear parents of blessed memory, Mazi Lambert S. Ekechukwu and Nwugo Caroline Ekechukwu, as well as all those patriots who have paid various prices for the good of Nigeria.

TABLE OF CONTENTS

In ECHOES FROM NIGERIA, written in distinct and peculiar language structure, the Author did a fantastic job of interweaving the role Leadership plays in the descent of a State into failure and collapse and the resulting notable issues like security gap, capacity gap and legitimacy gap etc. Suggesting solutions, ECHOES FROM NIGERIA tried to recreate the Nigerian nation while offering us great hope for a better tomorrow.

Great job Nwodibo Ekechukwu. Congratulations.

— **Professor (Noble Lady) Viola Adaku Onwuliri,** FNSBMB, FNISEB, FWIMA, FHOESON, ALOHA, LKSJI, *Former Hon. Minister of State 1 and Supervising Minister Foreign Affairs & Former Minister of State Education, Nigeria*

PREFACE

Echoes from Nigeria is a collection of poems that cuts across various genres. It attempts to capture some happenings in our beloved country, Nigeria, from precolonial times to the present period. Mirroring a society as large and complex as Nigeria can be challenging. Glittering generalities have been employed, in many instances, for effect. Satire has been used where necessary.

Essentially, this work is an appeal to poetic emotions in relation to Nigeria, our nationhood, culture, environmental concerns, socio-economic issues, crime, insecurity, morality, religion, marriage, traditions, family values, folklore, oil and the Niger Delta as well as childhood foibles and nuances. There is a nostalgic recollection of our golden era and the need to right some present wrongs. It brings to the fore therefore some of our current social vices, creating awareness on the various scourges, while trying to offer solutions.

Efforts have been made to write each poem in four verses for every stanza. The employment of rhymes and rhythm is to deepen the poetic effects. This collection is considered appropriate for undergraduates, senior high school students and general readership. It is hoped that it will be of value to anyone desirous of increasing his or her knowledge, and vocabulary of the issues embodied in the poems.

I thank most immensely my wife and children for their support, for bearing with my less attention to them in the course of writing these poems. I appreciate the efforts of my Computer Operator, Mr. Clinton Chiedozie Nwokocha, for typing the manuscript.

THE FORCED POLYGAMIST

Ugo loves his wife
He really enjoys his life
Four years ago they tied the nuptial knot
It took place in a beautiful city in the North

It was a high society wedding
No hitch, the organisers need not wade in
It is a marriage the couple truly treasure
They've been having great pleasure

They had a wonderful meetaversary
It was a well-celebrated dateaversary
The fourth anniversary of their wedding, low-keyed
They deliberately ensured it was monkeyed

Their marriage comes under intense pressure
They experience anguish in a great measure
Busybodies are terming them childless
The man really cares less

Her mother-in-law casts furtive glances at her tummy
It is as if she is now a subject in anatomy
She has remained slim with flat belly
The mother-in-law wants to see a potbelly

She wants to see her grandchildren
Uncomfortable with a woman that seems barren
She advises her son to jettison monogamy
She says their culture allows polygamy
The pressure on the couple is so unbearable

It makes them greatly miserable
The man loves his wife
He does not want his family in strife

Every morning his mother brings up the issue
She won't give respite to a couple without an issue
This is really tormenting him
He no longer enjoys his morning hymn

Gossips and side remarks in the town are rife
He eventually bows to pressure and takes a second wife
Soon after, the first wife delivers
Her womb is indeed a conceiver's

CIRCUMCISE NOT OUR FEMALES

They awaited the native midwife
She then arrives with her crude knife
The purpose is Ada's circumcision
The eight-day-old girl is to undergo incision

The innocent baby, unaware of the glances of murder
It is calmly cuddled by her mother
Why have we not completely overgrown this culture?
Why are females still undergoing this torture?

The elders say it reduces sexual sensitivity
They want to prevent promiscuity
The campaign by the authorities is not heeded
They say the campaign is not needed

Untrained native midwives become surgeons
They are operating female children in dungeons
The outcome is uncertain
That the instruments are crude is certain

Not only are the instruments crude
The midwife's attitude is also rude
The cries of the baby attract no sympathy
The midwife carries on without empathy

The prohibition is in the law books
It is also condemned by the holy guidebooks
The authorities should put their feet down
Let there be a clampdown

THE TENTH CHILD TROPHY

The trophy is a goat
It is still a practice for which a few gloat
They are yielding tenaciously to tradition
Their belief, enhanced by superstition

A mother is under a heavy burden
She is to bear ten children
Bringing her to the circle of fruitful femininity
Those in the group relish their fertility

A family becomes more than a football team
Raising the children, now a tall dream
Gone are the days a family needed many farm hands
Machines can now do all the work no matter how big
the farm lands

By Mbaise old tradition, when one was raised, one
would bring up all others
Present realities may not admit of such ancestral
orders
We should therefore put behind our ego
Our time is different from decades ago

Where lies the wisdom of the tenth child trophy?
It is now more of an atrophy
Let us emulate countries of the West
They do not kill any goat for the waist

Even the polygamists should also consider family
planning

Self-regulation is more appropriate than Government banning

Then problem with such a law will be the difficulty in enforcement

There may also be illegal abortifacient

THE GODS WERE STOLEN

For over a century the gods had been there
Da Njoku, the Chief Priest, held them so dear
He inherited them from his father
His father took over from his forefather

They resided in front of his compound, in a hut
We saw them through small openings, afraid we
could be hurt
They were assorted wooden carvings with different
engravings
Their sight fed our pastime and cravings

They were all engulfed in dust
Some were almost turning to crust
For how long they had been there only God knew
However their antique appearance was in view

The mud hut had a thatched roof
Under it, the gods had always stood aloof
They had remained motionless
There was no sign of life in the god or goddess

At the entrance, outside, would often be some eggs,
kolanuts and native chalk
Whenever we passed, they would be objects of our
talk
Sometimes we would see a fat native cow
This would be another fortune-telling inflow

One morning Da Njoku went to the hut

He was sweating while the place was not hot
He had noticed footprints fading from afar
He then saw the door ajar

It was fairly dark
Why sweating while it was dank?
Some gods had been stolen
He was visibly crestfallen

He went around the village
Stopping at any point that was vintage
Declaring seven days for the gods to fight back
For a year the gods showed no whack

Some weeks later, the remaining gods were purloined
He was bewildered that the rest had been eloigned
The gods never avenged
No one at any time revenged

Some Christians at that point came, coincidentally
The gods Da Njoku worshipped were no more, incidentally
They had been stolen because of their golden antiquity
He became a Christian, after all the gods could not punish the iniquity

THE OSTRACISED

In Nigeria today, the rule of law prevails
However, in some places, ostracism still assails
It was a means of social control pre-colonialism
It should have no place in constitutionalism

Our Forefathers used it to ensure peace and harmony
The non-conformists suffered the agony
The Nigerian communities then were also organised
Errant members were duly chastised

Ostracism was meted out for any heinous offence
For which the suspect offered no acceptable defence
This included anyone who broke a taboo
He would inescapably meet his waterloo

Murder, incest, adultery, stealing, poisoning and
treachery would occasion ostracism
This stemmed from the society's value of altruism
No member of the community would have any dealing
with him
It would be immaterial that he had been forgiven by
the victim

Typically, when a person is ostracized, no one talks to
him or any of his relations
He neither buys from nor sells anything to any person
in the habitations
No one renders him any assistance in times of need
If he cries for help no one will heed

In extreme cases, in the past, the ostracised would be
sent into exile
He was bound to find his new environment hostile
Today, ostracism still has its subtle vestiges
There are numerous menaces

THE TOWN'S DISPUTES, THE KING'S GAIN

The people chose him as their king
The contest was so keen
They saw him as their saviour
They disliked other contestants' behaviour

The king weekly holds court
The venue is the king's court
He does this with his council of chiefs
Clad in red caps, beads and neckerchiefs

The king-in-council hears the complainants and defendants
In the presence of all the attendants
Each party presents kolanuts, kegs of wine and a goat
These are things over which the king and his chiefs gloat

The items are taken during the mediation
The remains are the king's ingratiation
The palace store is fuller with more disputes
This is because of more edible and drinkable inputs

These can be further augmented
Fines on the defaulting party, are never contested
They are lesser than heavier punishments
Heinous acts attract ostracism or banishments

THE PALACE GUARDS

They are with the king always
They serve him in many ways
They make sure he is secure
Whatever he wants they procure

They sit on the floor of the palace
They attend to him when he is seated in his place
They sing his praise
At intervals their voices raise

They are his guard of honour
They are his suppliers of humour
They are his drummers
They are jesters and singers

They are all in their flowing gowns
Both the palace and guards, the king owns
The king cannot be harmed
The guards are armed

Their swords are in their sheaths
They are battle-ready even when they leave the floor
for their seats
They spring up when the king is attacked
They will ensure the attacker is counterattacked

THE CROWN FELL INTO A GUTTER

Everywhere in the world the crown is revered
Instead of losing it, a king may have his head severed
The king is made by the crown
So it is esteemed in every town

Those who are made kings are carefully selected
In some communities they are elected
The Government then approves and gives staff of authority
Where the Government disapproves, the process is started afresh by the community

The king first wears the crown during coronation
This is the case even if he emerges through agnation
He equally receives his staff of office
For his enthronement this will suffice

It is definitely a sacred calling
A king must therefore avoid any falling
Kings rarely eat in public
Even when the country is a republic

The king's discipline transcends his kingdom
It is also immaterial that his is a fiefdom
The subjects were alarmed to see the king engage his wife in a street fight
Those at the scene were filled with fright

The king and the queen were in a brawl
The king fell and was in a sprawl

He had accused her of unroyal conduct
He would not stomach the misconduct

The crown fell into a gutter
Those watching did not know what to utter
They were in shock and disbelief
They would look up to the Government for relief

Truly the Government wielded the big stick
It was indeed quick
The king was dethroned
Another person was enthroned

He was banished to another town
He went, wearing not a crown but a frown
There he is under a king
He is also without any kith and kin

THE KING OF ALL NUTS

Nigeria's kola tree bears the king nut
It is eaten so much in the North
It is celebrated in the East
It is served in every feast

The kolanut is grown mainly in the West
This is a fact to which many will attest
It is used for any traditional occasion
This is the case in Nigeria, wherever the location

The Hausas do not engage in fanfare before they eat
it
The Yorubas will have the king bless it before they
eat
Different ethnic groups exhibit to it their peculiar
attitude
The Igbos, however, take it to a higher altitude

They say it does not hear English
They bless it in their language with relish
The presentation of kolanut in any event is significant
To set the right mood, it is needed as a lubricant

This is done by the Chief Host giving it to the royal or
elderly
It must be a person of his community, related
brotherly
The receiver, accordingly, informs the guests
Their faces beam as they watch with interests

It is frowned at to ignore any notable person
The receiver ensures all relevant guests acknowledge
seeing the nut(s), including the chairperson
He blesses it, praying for the success of the occasion
He dilutes his prayers at intervals with an exclamation

The nuts are broken for all to chew
In all these, if there is a mistake the process starts
anew
A slip can be failing to give each community one to
take home
It can also be not recognizing notable persons with
some

This can lead to loud protests until it is addressed
Occasionally, there will be a suspension of the
programme until it is redressed
The defaulting party may pay a fine
A long delay can definitely remove the event's shine

SWEAR AND TAKE

A piece of land in the village can give rise to dispute
There will be efforts at mediation by men of repute
These men include the disputing parties' male kiths and kin
If it is unresolved, the matter goes to the king

They may still be irreconcilable at the king's court
The conduct of one of them may be so curt
The king will then subject the willing party to oath-taking
This is normally a very solemn step thoughtfully taken

It is done with fetish objects, a deity or a Holy Book
Sometimes the swearing party will fear he will be caught by the hook
The person administering it normally states the rules
It is among his schedules

For the next one year the parties will neither eat nor drink together
This is to void the likelihood of poisoning or any blither
The essence again is to know when nemesis strikes
Action by God Almighty or the deity must be distinguished from phantom-likes

Death occurring in a party's family within the period signifies a false swearing
If it occurs after one year it is deemed to have no bearing

There is a celebration whenever there is no death
The land then becomes theirs after that date

THE FRAUDSTERS

Their tongues are coated with sugar
Beneath each is actually a dagger
Their pens are prolific
The harm is often horrific

Their methods are many
They can sometimes also be uncanny
Their victims are in all climes
Location does not really matter in their crimes

They churn out daily, hundreds of emails
Many of them, of course, are males
Their smartphones are often their major tools
With them they make their victims fools

They sometimes initiate a scam through personal contact
This they do with so much tact
It can be through an initial phone call
Blame yourself also if you fall

Computer manipulation by them is rife
This recently cost a man his life
They stole all his information
He died from subsequent deformation

They are experts in identity theft
They get information by means so deft
They can access information on a bank account
They will then clear all the amount

Be wary of unsolicited assistance
They will not succeed when there is resistance
Do not lend yourself to their creed
They feast on any prospective victim's greed

THIS HOUSE IS NOT FOR SALE

"Beware of 419. This House is Not for Sale"
Property-related fraud is on a large scale
Such kind of inscription on some buildings is very common
For likely intending buyers, it is to forewarn

This is more noticeable in an urban or semi urban area
The public is alerted to have an idea
The catch phrase is "Buyer Beware"
A house is not for sale and the public should be aware

Fraudsters are on the loose
If you are not careful with your money you will lose
Prospective house buyers must avoid being duped
The money may not be recouped

Scammers present houses for sale, unknown to the owners
Buyers must ensure they identify the actual homeowners
This is a way of avoiding becoming victims
Conducts with due diligence will save purchasers from fraudsters' whims

Buyers must watch out for documents cloned
The crooks present documents ingeniously honed
Intending buyers should run away from such titles
This is to avoid losing money and litigation battles

What properly confer ownership of a house to a person are relevant documents
Whosoever purportedly buys any house without such has nothing without the instruments
419 is a Section on obtaining by false pretenses in the criminal code
It is about the ingredients of the offence and the fraudsters' mode

Fraudsters are clever
They know how to maneuver
They take the intended victims to the house location
They make sure the homeowner will not be around during the inspection

Within the premises they may have an accomplice
He will play the script of the required service
Beware when therefore you see "This House is Not for Sale"
Keep your money so that you will not have a sorry tale

WHY DIE IN SILENCE?

Occasionally in a place you see a "Mystery, Mystery" sign board
"Why Die In Silence?" is the writing in concord
Oftentimes there is a picture of a mermaid-like woman
Rarely is it that of a man

A big snake coils round her neck
This apparently is an illustration of power and a roughneck
The contact address is a dingy room
There, there is all the evidence of gloom

Sometimes there is also an advert in other obscure media
It requests the reader to contact a 'doctor' often linked to India
He is supposedly a 'guru' in magical power
People are expected to cower

His power, ostensibly derived from the mermaid or India is portrayed as guaranteeing riches
It is obvious that riches are outside his own reaches
He will give 'a magical pen' to pass examinations
He never passed any and has no certificates

He promises 'Touch and Follow', 'Love Portion'
His wife has abandoned him for lack of affection
He advertises cure for every illness
However, he is sick and appears helpless

He assures good luck
His life radiates lack
Yes, you do not need to die in silence
Look up instead for divine omnipotence

NIGERIA'S SOCIAL MEDIA AS LOOSE CANNONS

Decades ago Marshall McLuhan called the world a global village
Today the world is becoming a family assemblage
This is because of the ease, speed and spread of the social media
The Nigerian situation appears to be more of a crazy multimedia

The creators of social media intended them to be of positive mass communication
The abuses have turned them into an aberration
Our regular media are regulated
The social media are virtually unregulated

There are so many lies posted on Facebook
Through Facebook meeting, a lady was lured and killed by a crook
A lot of falsehood has been circulated through WhatsApp
To many people obsessed by it, it has become a trap

Some followers have been misled by postings on Instagram
Students more pre-occupied with social media failed their exam
Some job seekers have been duped through LinkedIn
They realized this too late, to their chagrin

The internet is an awesome creation

It is a great vehicle for communication and education
Government must, however, seriously check the abuses
Emplacing legislations and institutions can stop misuses

THE AREA BOYS

They are brazen street urchins
Some have scars from bloody fights in their chins
They operate in groups
They may also dwindle into in-groups

It is not often difficult to know them
Their eyes are blood-shot as some suffer exanthem
They are dirty and scruffy
Their hair is dandruffy

Their stock in trade is brazen extortion
Any attempt at resistance attracts dispersion
These vagabonds make demands with menaces
Their operations are common in market places

One is at risk if one is well-dressed
Similarly, one is in danger if kempt and one's dress
properly pressed
Bags, handsets, wristwatches and jewelries are their
attractions
Some victims will be happy for suffering only few
subtractions

Some shop owners do not want their everyday
molestation
They pay 'security fees' monthly and avoid daily
contestation
They will enjoy 'free' loading and offloading of their
goods
Those not subscribing can lose their livelihoods

THE BLACK MARKETS

Both day and night they are operated
They thrive on colours whose prices are regulated
The sellers and buyers have one thing in common
They are not governed by official rates and action

The foreign currency market is the most notorious
The fuel market, especially during scarcity, is famous
The Government calls the shadowy currency
exchange transactions the 'parallel market'
It is difficult to regulate those involved in the racket

Many black marketers do not have registered offices
They are under trees, by some streets in open places
Buyers from them want convenience, quickness and
secrecy
There is no form of bureaucracy

For fuel, anywhere can be a black market
The fuel or gas station can also become one in
alternate
Road sides are no exception
Petrol black markets thrive in scarcity situation

The Government agencies' efforts at raiding have not
achieved much
It is a supply and demand match
Solutions may lie in the adequacy of foreign exchange
and fuel
Otherwise, inadequacy will continue to create a
situation that is so cruel

VICTIMS OF UNCERTAIN JOURNEYS

The pictures of the destination are painted rosy
The environment is glorified as cozy
Few earlier sojourners returned and built houses
Victims are often unaware they are meant for whorehouses

Their ordeal commences with the Sahara Desert—Libya journey
It is highly risky, tortuous and life-threatening, in jitneys
Sixty persons may be cramped in a vehicle meant for twenty
Occupants drink their urine and sometimes throw out the *fainty*

It is therefore a survival of the fittest
This is a situation all lovers of decency must detest
Sugar-coated mouths lure victims with bogus claims
Prospective victims never know the real aims

Oaths of allegiance are administered in fearful shrines
Victims agree to pay fees in cash and of all kinds
Being vulnerable, they consent in unquestioning submission
They will be imagining pictures of a bountiful mission

Parents in peer competition are complicit
This is even when the evils of the journey are explicit
Some ignorantly rejoice that their child is going oversea

They are unaware of constant deaths in the
Mediterranean Sea

The hellish Niger-Desert-Libya trip is but the first leg
The sail across the Mediterranean is as delicate as
walking on raw eggs
Many drown en masse
And the bereaved can only celebrate requiem mass

THE PALM-HOLD FUFU: A METAPHOR FOR CORRUPTION

They are children of the same family
They eat from one bowl chummily
Inspiring great amity
A source of unity

Each eater is however expected to be considerate
One should only take what is commensurate
This involves a sense of moderation
It is not about how hungry one is, but the need to ration

Children are moulded from infancy to care
They, from infancy, imbibe the spirit to always share
Where they do not assimilate this habit, greed rules
It becomes a survival for the fittest and the attendant ridicules

The meal of fufu and soup so illustrates
The soup and fufu are put in separate plates
One cuts a size of the fufu with one's palm
The portion is then reduced to morsels with the other arm

In cutting, a greedy person can take very disproportionately
Thus in comparison to others he cuts inordinately
This palm-hold gluttony is corruption
It is indeed unfair to wallow in selfish consumption

THE STREET HAWKERS

They are on major roads in any big city
Hawking on the streets constitutes a constant irregularity
The hawkers are like bees on hives of any traffic gridlock
Their presence constitutes a roadblock

They hawk anything, from human-size mirrors to snacks
Among them are many marketing quacks
They don't have shops due to lack of the wherewithal
Should they pay for shops they will not have any capital

The Environmental Protection Agency occasionally conducts a raid
The hawkers at such times see red
Some of them are caught
Then they are charged to court

They are often fined
Some are discharged if the magistrate is so kind
It is unclear what happens to the items
It appears they melt away in the systems

This is because no one has ever heard of their public auction
No one has also witnessed their combustion
The Government should empower these hawkers with free small shops

This will enable them get their daily sops

THE TRAFFIC JAM

I ran into a terrific traffic jam
I was on my way to a site to pick Mr. Sam
A narrow two-way thoroughfare
Certainly not good for a funfair

I stretched my eyes beyond my sight
And beheld a stream of vehicles on the site
Behind me was fully clogged
The entire road was thronged

The blazing sun was at its peak
I was afraid my radiator would leak
The heat was unbearable
I am not speaking in parable

Disorderliness had set in
I sought for an inn
I wanted to have some rest
My wish to keep away from the pest

The cacophonous honks were deafening
The beads of sweat on many faces, overwhelming
Many lost their voices in abuses as the traffic started
crawling
Some motorists were just drawling

THE GIRL IN MINI SKIRT AND THE MARKET WOMEN

Yesterday the girl left the town
She came to Ogwu, a village of her own
She then went to her first target
This was the village market

She wanted to pick few things
She had, before returning, gotten some tins
She came out of the car
Some market women had seen her from afar

The girl, a graduate, was in miniskirt
They therefore branded her a flirt
She was taken aback
She was surprised at their verbal attack

They were hurling at her insults
She could not comprehend such reactions from adults
She heard the jeers
The whole air, rent in sneers

She hurried to her car and drove away
Where she went to they were unaware
Then she came back with the Police
The verbal abusers she had taken notice

They were charged with defamation
They pleaded legitimation
They admitted being in the market scene

They questioned their offence in condemning what they considered obscene

OUTLANDISH FASHION

We look back, laugh and wonder
How come we ever wore certain things as fashion, we
ponder
Today wearing such will be unimaginable
It will, in fact, be totally inconceivable

Seeing some old photographs now evokes indignation
All one sees is sheepish fashion beyond imagination
From hair to toe a man looks out of the ordinary
His afro hair is bushy and appears unsanitary

He also wears oversized eyeglasses, branded
sunshades
He puts on a blowy shirt or jacket of lengthy collar
blades
He stands on multi-layered mountainous shoes
The wearer must be watching his gait and toes

What is in vogue relates to fashion
Modesty, convenience and suitability should be part
of our passion
Importation of styles from other climes may not
always make sense
What suits our bodies and is presentable makes
commonsense

THE MAD MAN'S MASOCHISM

On a madman's head is a heavy load
He moves slowly along the road
It is a load of useless nondescript items
All are packed in disorderly systems

It is a load he gave himself
It is an unnecessary burden itself
The sun is scorching
His whole body, bescorching

He sports his head of semi-dreadlocks
Multiple lies find habitation in the locks
He drops on the road, his beads of sweat
It seems to be his familiar beat

How did he lift the weighty basket?
It is not in any way a flasket
How does he bring it down?
It cannot be on his head from dusk to dawn

The state should save the mad man
Yes, she certainly can
This can be done by first ending this masochism
Thereafter he should be treated with humanism

BETRAYERS

They have been there since creation
Among the twelve apostles, Judas committed the abomination
The Holy Books contain many examples
No one should therefore trust all his disciples

They are in every sphere of life
A man can even be betrayed by his wife
Jesus in his divine wisdom foretold his
He knew that with man something could go amiss

A reformer will attract hatred
From those who do not hold good virtues sacred
They pray for the God-fearing to give away
They will want to continue iniquity by holding sway

Pray they do not have opportunity to blackmail
They will brandish enormous lies and assail
Slow poisons will bare their fangs
They will even enlist other gangs

When their negative interests are touched, they go mad
They will then pay good with bad
For crossing their paths they search for scapegoats
All over the place will be turncoats

Blessed be leaders who fear God
They will always disappoint those who cod
Above all, we will all face divine judgement

There will be no escape from reward or punishment

A FATHER'S STRUGGLE

It is a carryover of the Biblical and the Qu'ranic scene
It is like a manifestation of God's rage over Adamic sin
A man has to provide his family needs
He has to ensure his family feeds

A man must struggle
He must haggle
It has become his lot
He cannot give excuse of any sort

The father is a bread winner
So he provides breakfast, lunch and dinner
He is the family's paramount provider
Exuding the true qualities of a leader

In his home he is the major voice
The decisions he makes are his choice
He is, of course, the stronger vessel
But he must sometimes seek wise counsel

The wife is also an important partner
Her supporting role makes things easier
Together they build the family
They and the children will benefit continually

A MOTHER'S LOVE

A mother's love for her baby is unquantifiable
It is also in the positive sense not qualifiable
From conception to delivery she cares
From birth to adulthood she spares

She endures a lot of discomfort
While trying to give her baby comfort
She keeps awake until it sleeps
She carries it well, lest it slips

She constantly breastfeeds it
She cuddles it from birth to weaning as it begins to
eat
Her care starts right from the day of its birth
She routinely gives it a tender bath

She rocks it to slumber
She pampers it even as it tries to cumber
She, with it, establish a sign language
Its mood becomes easy for her to gauge

It is amazing the insane also show motherly care
They are ready to die for their babies, the way other
mothers are
There is a story of the depraved who concealed a
pregnancy
She always strapped, very tightly, her abdomen, in
secrecy

On delivery, she ensured the baby was cast away

Later in life she regretted making it a castaway
Sometimes, divorce shoves a mother aside
This may follow a man's preference for a younger
bride

She still cares for the children
This she does in the sun and in the rain
Let's appreciate motherhood
It is something beyond womanhood

THE HAPPY COUPLE

A happy home is always the dream of any lady
Especially when she is marriage-ready
She wants to settle down in a happy family
She works towards this sincerely

This applies also to a prospective husband
He yawns for a good wife in a land
He has the same mindset
He works towards it from the outset

This is not about having enormous wealth
It is also not about a perfect health
It is not about the lady being a beauty queen
The man also needs not be the most handsome king

It has to do with planning
It involves a form of learning
There must be sacrifice
Love and understanding will suffice

There will be times of gains
There will also be moments of pains
It will not be always smooth
It is not every time it will soothe

The couple has to remain focused
Whatever is confusing should be discussed
This is to avoid misunderstanding
They should strive for oneness, the storms in life
notwithstanding

They should put their trust in the Almighty God
They should not hope on any demi-god
Prayers can make a difference
God will surely order their preference

THE JOY OF THE PARENTS

Parents make the upbringing of their children a
priority
They deny themselves comfort in frugality
For them it is a matter of deferred gratification
The children are expected in their later stage to show
appreciation

The children, in adulthood, will nourish their parents
They will shower them with presents
They will exhibit manifest care
They will ensure their parents have good healthcare

They will protect the family's name
This is by good conduct and everything sane
In our country old people's home is virtually alien
Familial contacts and bonds should not be broken

Children are the biggest insurance for old age
"He who has people is bigger than the wealthy" says
our adage
A caregiver may not perform that role more than
one's blood
The difference is in the sublime and psychological
flood

All the children may not give parents equal attention
For each, it all depends on the level of affection
This is further influenced by his or her capacity
There will also be obvious differences in their ability

The spirit is what matters
It will be obvious when one caters
The metamorphosis of humans should be explained to
them to know
The offspring of today are, of course, the parents of
tomorrow

THE OVERWORKED HOUSEMAID

She woke early
She has hardly slept well lately
She has to attend to every domestic chore
She has unwittingly become the household's core

She ate the left-over at noon, breaking her unwitting fast
She, of course, hardly has breakfast
She first has to clean the house and bathe madam's children
She then tends the large garden in sun or rain

A mountain of clothes awaits her laundry
She keeps washing until the taps run dry
Her name is the most called in the household
Different members give her tasks some beyond a ten-year old

Dirty kitchen utensils and plates keep accumulating
When she would wash them is what she is contemplating
She awaits the weekend to wash her only dress
She washes it in midnight for less stress

She ties a wrapper before it dries
All these she does in her silent cries
Her parents had been promised a lot
What she is going through is a sad lot for a mere tot

She is yet to resume the evening class

Her time for this is for her cutting grass
Neighbors do not want to speak out
They are afraid of what may be the fallout

THE UNFORTUNATE ORPHAN

The parents died in one-year interval
Since then it has been a struggle for survival
He was nine when first his father died
He really uncontrollably cried

The tears had not dried
The same year the mother died
He was an only child
He has become forcibly mild

His uncle has moved into their house
This, for the orphan, is a major grouse
He has given each of his five children a room
He shares with his wife the master bedroom

It is a six bedroom modern apartment
They are reveling in contentment
They are visibly gloating
The orphan is floating

The uncle and his family used to live in a mud
structure
They now know the difference in architecture
They love their own children
They treat the orphan like somebody barren

He is in their bondage
Who will deliver him from this hostage?
Being in his infancy he is powerless
When food is served he is given less

He has not been to school for one session
The couple has taken all his father's possession
He prays for their change of heart every day
God, he believes, will surely answer him someday

THE BRIDE AS TROPHY

A man has proposed to a woman
There is also a proposal from another man
The woman has a choice
But tradition makes her not have a voice

This tradition of time immemorial minimally prevails
Who marries her depends on who this avails
The two men must engage in a wrestling contest
Who becomes her husband takes her for conquest

The bride is the prize
She is to be won not by what is paid as price
She is coveted by the winner of the wrestling match
The two suitors rarely mismatch

The difference may not be in who has greater muzzle
He is not to effectively exert his muscle
He must, however, have sharp fighting skills
This is not to say that he has to wrestle his opponent
with overkills

The whole essence is to ensure he is hardworking
He should feed his family even if it is through eking
He should have the power to defend his family
He has to always protect them firmly

The villagers form a circle around
The winner emerges by throwing his opponent on the
ground
A wrestler should not suffer any form of atrophy

If he does, he can easily be beaten by his opponent, who takes the bride as a trophy

THE ALMAJIRIS

They should all be respected Qur'anic students in the society
Some have, however, become destitute urchins deserving of our piety
They carry pans in their hands
This is caused by poverty in our lands

These children should be in school
Often times, they instead muster in the beggars' pool
Some are in the hands of wrong teachers
Their parents do not always monitor the preachers

The teachers collect the begging proceeds
The Almajiri eats if in the day's begging he succeeds
Then you ask, what are their goals?
Will their progress in life not suffer heavy tolls?

To these children the nation should give a serious thought
If we deny them western education, additionally, we are liable of a tort
Such education will make them more enlightened
Their horizon will be better widened

They will become more useful citizens
They will be respected denizens
They will no more be willing tools
They will not yield to negative uses by crooks

THE STATION TEACHER

He lives in the school premises
He is the bad pupils' nemesis
He is in-charge after school, though he is one of the masters
He keeps an eye on the school and its quarters

One must not be around ten minutes after the dismissal hymn
Any erring pupil will have to explain why, to him
He wields a lengthy cane
So be careful not to cross his lane

Venture not around the mango tree
Otherwise, whatever your explanation is he will disagree
It is immaterial whether a mango is up or fell
Your answer will fail

You will be called out next morning as the pupils assemble
When you hear your name you will tremble
You will surely be caned
This is to ensure you are tamed

RESPECT FOR ELDERS

Respect for elders is virtually a universal phenomenon
For all ethnic groups in Nigeria, it is common
In western nations it is ethical
In Nigeria, it is cultural

Western countries pay more emphasis on respect for
the elderly whether or not they are denizens
Passengers in a bus or train are urged to yield seats
to senior citizens
In Africa or Nigeria it is about being older
The exception may be when the younger person is a
higher officer holder

In Northern Nigeria, juniors greet seniors with
clenched fists, slightly bowing
In the west it involves sometimes prostrating or
stooping
In the east it is expressed more verbally
Various groups often greet traditionally

It is part of the general Nigerian tradition to yield a
seat to a much older person
In buses and trains this is, however, uncommon
This is when it is a situation of first-come-first-served
Yielding seats in such a circumstance, to some
appears undeserved

WALKING STICKS FOR ALL

They used to be for the elderly and infirm
This was in the days of yore, in Igboland, I can confirm
Today walking sticks have become fashionable
Previously, among the Igbos, for the young and healthy, they were untouchable

It is now the new fashion craze in our clime
It was never like that in earlier time
Then in Igboland they were for those above seventy years
Now the young men who carry them worsen our fears

The fears are that they are being influenced by fashion elsewhere
It is not just about copying fashion from somewhere
The issue is throwing a privilege of the elderly to all-comers
We resent this aping of fashion of all manners

Admittedly the Ijaws sometimes wield sticks while dancing
It is used by the Fulanis in herding
It is therefore not just about the stick
It is the issue of carrying it as a fashion pick.

For the Kalabaris it is part of their men's dressing
For the Urhobos, Efiks, Ibibios and Annangs without it, their apparels will not be arresting
Yes, culture is dynamic

This is more so in a country like ours that is multiethnic

WE ARE BLESSED

Nigeria is a blessed country
We have a rich ancestry
We are the biggest black nation
This started from the 1914 amalgamation

We cherish our October 1, 1960 independence
Let us continue to consolidate it by interdependence
Our strength lies in our unity
Our unity thrives in patriotism and amity

We are blessed with diverse cultures
Evident in our carnivals and festivals features
They make us outstanding in nations' comity
They project us in the international community

We must hold tight our freedom
Let's continue to nourish it with tact and wisdom
We should do away with any form of bigotry
Let's worship God truly and avoid idolatry

We must remain grateful to God for arable lands
He has also given us capable hands
Let us pile up mountains of cash crops
We should also sustain the efforts so that there will
be no drops

We have enough aquatic riches
Properly harnessed, we can eat and export fishes
We have a flourishing vegetation
This should be guarded through proper conservation

We have good climate
Nature has made it temperate
We have different seasons
We can, through irrigation, even plant preseasons

We have diverse mineral resources
Let's exploit them for more wealth-sources
Let's develop for tourism our multiple beaches
They should be veritable sources of our riches

We do not experience any earthquake
Volcanoes do not give us headache
What we witness, rarely, is flood
We should not therefore, on our own, shed blood

OUR YEARS OF INNOCENCE AND NOW

There was greater peace across Nigeria
Ethnic groups abounded but lived together in positive euphoria
Rarely were there issues involving people running helter-skelter
A harmonious existence made our nation greater

There was absence of deep-rooted rancor and bitterness
Then there existed only a mild semblance of suspicion and sinisterness
Today, in contrast, it is more of a hellish spectre of brutish violence
Our country is currently witnessing turbulence

Can we ever go back to yesteryears innocence?
Will we continue in this nonsense?
Do we fast and pray with incense?
How can we be properly guided by common sense?

Prayer must go with good work
Let's rebuild Nigeria on a unifying framework
The emphasis should be on nationalism
Both leaders and followers must be fired by patriotism

Let's fully restore our spirit of benevolence
We all must eschew hate-speech and insolence
No society has progressed with pervasive act of vengeance

Many nations excel by the large extent to which her people exhibit tolerance

SACREDNESS OF A NIGERIAN LIFE

The respect for the sacredness of life is universal
Humanity guards life jealously for survival
We are now witnessing the gradual erosion of the
sanctity of life
Persons and communities are being strafed by knives
and strife

Why are Nigerians being often brutally shot?
Why are lives being daily cut short?
The Nigerian life is that of a human
It is not that of any tree, crop, animal or any sub-
human

The lives of these, no doubt, also matter
Because humans depend on them for food on the
platter
God has given us dominion over other creatures
We know this, even without being told by preachers

The sacredness of man's life is therefore divine
The Nigerian constitution which prohibits unlawful
killing is in line
All religions decree respect for human life, with some
consequences afterlife
Our laws permit the killing of those who unlawfully
take life

The ceaseless orgy of large-scale killing we
sometimes now witness is very dangerous
It is not only unlawful, it is irreligious

It is an exercise in self-immolation
We must stop this movement to perdition

The nation must be united to stem this scourge
Every hand must be on deck to prevent a further surge
There should be no blame game
Any excuse in this direction will be lame

PEACE IN OUR LAND

We must guard our fortunes jealously
This we must also do zealously
Our oil should not be a curse
It should be our joyous cause

Our strength should lie in unity
There should be no cause for disunity
We seek a Niger Delta of our dream
It should be like a shiny cream

No one should steal our innocence
No person should harbor insolence
God bless our founding fathers
We should adorn their caps with feathers

They mithered the colonialists into submission
With independence they accomplished their mission
Those without oil live in peace
Our oil should not set us apiece

Are there those obsessed with agitation, insurgency
or freedom-fighting?
Let them shed no blood and be non-intimidating
There are alternatives to belligerency
Peaceful approaches should be preferred to militancy

Let peace reign in our land
Let law and order sound from our band
Violence or blood-letting abhor
Brotherhood and friendship adore

THE FARMERS AND HERDERS WE USED TO KNOW

It was a peaceful relationship
None was obsessed with killing over ownership
They had sanctity for life
No activities resulted to serious strife

The cows fed on uncultivated fields
Cow dungs deposited on fallow places would, when cultivated, increase yields
Their relationship was beneficial
The understanding was mutual

The farmers knew that they needed cow meat
The herders would also need farm yields to eat
The farmers at times provided land for temporary herders' shelter
The farmers sometimes also gave them water

The two groups would often times exchange harvests
Both farmers and herders were safe in the forests
Herders would herd their flock through many appropriate places unmolested
Where cows strayed and destroyed crops, the issue would be successfully arbitrated

The herders we knew carried only sticks and machetes
They were not known to carry even axes
The farmers worked with their machetes and hoes
They never saw the herders as foes

THE PEASANT FARMER

The farmer has tilled the ground
He expects for this season a major turnaround
He has, after the second rain planted his seeds
He hopes to eventually sell, profit and meet all his needs

Ordinarily, the raining season is from April to October
It is mid-April and he prays for harvest that will be a bumper
The Government has given him improved seedling
The authorities are now shifting emphasis to farming

An early planter harvests before the others
If drought sets in, great will be the loss he suffers
So he prays for continuous rainfall
This will guarantee him a windfall

He has heard of mechanized farming
Its yield will always be more accruing
The cost of mechanized farming is however prohibitive
Hiring of the equipment is also very expensive

Co-operatives of small farmers attract little facilities
Subsistence farmers lack funds for large-scale activities
The big ones are few
Other key players in the business are new

What is needed is an agricultural revolution

Everyone will be involved in its execution
Let's join hands to feed the nation
Everybody should have a ration

LESSONS FROM BED BUGS

We have some lessons to learn from some insects
These issues are of various aspects
Take for instance, the bed bug
Its attitude to a hot water spray is smug

This has become proverbial
It tells its nymphs not to react to the adversarial
It says they should not panic when poured water that is hot
It urges them to remain steadfast, as they will be unhurt

The bug and its nymphs normally reside in bed crevices
They creep out to suck the blood of any person on the bed, through his epidermis
For centuries ago our people battled them with hot water
The bed bug said it did not matter

It told the nymphs to be calm
It said there would be no qualm
It hinged this on the fact that what was hot would become cold
This made them bold

This is certainly a lesson in patience
An undue haste can be destructive and amounts to impatience
The bed bug survived because it remained stoic

It exists today because, in such situations, it was stolidly anesthetic

Today they are still in some beds' underside
They have not been completely eradicated by insecticide
Efforts at killing them have been constant
Some of them have, in some homes, remained resistant

LESSONS FROM ANTS

We all know that ants are social
To them individual living is antisocial
They live in colonies
They move in companies

Proverbially, they say that whoever disorganizes their
movement does so in vain
This is because they will realign and move forward
like a train
This is a lesson in perseverance
It is an attitude of endurance

There is also the issue of life in a community
There are advantages with the associated comity
Their strength is in their unity
Their survival is in their affinity

The ants are always determined to reach their
destination
They know there can be an interruption
This will make them to scatter
Thereafter they will muster

They will continue united in their march
This is the situation even if they are ascending a larch
It is a forward movement
They are undeterred by the interrupting moment

TORTOISE'S THREE HUNDRED AND SIXTY FIFTH DAY IMPATIENCE

The tortoise was thrown into a deep hole for 364
days, unattended
It was a hole full of excreta as intended
Rescuers came on the 365th day
Help was coming its way

Tortoise, however, became very restless
It made the rescuers speechless
They were wondering what its haste was
Before then, for many months people would see it
and just pass

Its complaint was that the smell of the excreta was
unbearable
But it had endured it for a period unimaginable
The rescuers could not understand this last day
impatience
For tortoise it was no more a day of patience

There laid its lack of perseverance
What was required was a little more endurance
The haste it demanded could lead to its fatality
Rescuers were more concerned with its vivacity

THE CALABAR MAIDEN

She comes out of the fattening room
Every man will want to be her groom
It's been six months of heavy eating
She has grown in size by sumptuous feasting

She glows with her body so supple
Her new dress is very purple
Her hair is styled in twelve mushroom shapes
Each cluster of hairs is held by tiny black tapes

Beads adorn her neck, legs and one hand
She is so plump to behold in her homeland
She looks more like a well-fed teen
She is a bridal queen

The fattening is designed by parents
It is to make a girl marriageable as perceived by the
culture adherents
To them the negative health implications matter not
Talks about the isolation involved as an abuse often
come to naught

ONE MAN'S MEAT, ANOTHER'S POISON

Loving animals as pets is human
The dog is the best animal friend of man
In our nation some still hate it
This is because of the rabies it may transmit

Others cringe at the fact that some local breeds eat faeces
When you therefore mention dog, they are full of hisses
To the haters of the dog meat, the eaters should be tabooed
To the lovers it is the best food

The dog meat in some parts of Nigeria is a local delicacy
The lovers boast of its over-delicacy
They savour it as nutritious
They proclaim it as delicious

The connoisseurs prefer it as peppersoup
The chili and other condiments make it a spicy soup
It is a delight at drinking joints
The gourmets there make strong points

Indeed one man's meat is another's poison
No one has died from this bouillon
It is therefore a matter of choice
Everyone has a right to rejoice

THE FISHERMAN'S SOUP

The okro in the soup is sparse
This is not because it is scarce
The fisherman has the final say
He decides the quantity when making his soup for the
day

The fish in it is plenty
Without it the plate will be virtually empty
Periwinkles, crayfish, crabs and shrimps improve the
delicacy
A sprinkling of palm oil adds fancy

It is everybody's food
It is healthy and does everyone good
The fisherman merely eats part of his catch
Some tourists buy and eat in their yacht

Not everyone in the city affords it
The rich buy as much as they want to eat
Anyone that wants it should be ready to pay the price
It really tastes so nice

THE JOURNEY BY TRAIN

I remember our early years in the primary school in
Jos, Nigeria
It is indeed a feeling of great nostalgia
We looked forward to the schools vacating
The journeys by train from Jos to the East were
fascinating

Holidaying in the village kept us in tune with home
We suffered no absence-of-township-setting
syndrome
We gained a lot moving round
There was much assimilation from the environment
and people around

The greater pleasure was, however, in the journey
itself
The experience could be better described by oneself
The vibrating horn at the train terminal signaled
departure
This would be the beginning of the adventure

The train would then snake out in its many coaches
One would notice iron barricades by road
intersections in its approaches
These were to prevent intrusions on its track
A train could stop but I never saw one backtrack

A journey to Umuahia took two days
There was time to eat, sleep and look sideways
The sound of the engine provided good rhythm

It was as if it was accompanied with lyricism

I could remember some of the stations we passed
(Kafanchan, Lafia, Akwanga, Makurdi, Enugu) were
traversed
At such stations some passengers also disembarked
or embarked
Some would make purchases as the train parked

The most momentous part is the eye-feasting
Trees and houses would appear to be moving as the
train was advancing
In my ignorance I loved the soot from the locomotive
I now know the 'pleasant' smell can be linked to
illness as a causative

THE CHRISTMAS RICE

We used to eat rice then twice a year
These were on Christmas and New Year
We heard that those in townships ate it every Sunday
It is a staple food now, eaten by many every day

We used to yearn particularly for the Christmas rice
There was this childhood feeling that it tasted so nice
Imported long grained rice was unknown
What was available was the short grain, locally grown

Preparing it for cooking was however cumbersome
Removing the pebbles and sand was burdensome
Visible ones were first picked out
The rice would then be parboiled as a cookout

The remaining sand was removed through sieving
It was then boiled until ready for serving
The stew was always very aromatic
This was so whether it was from the kitchen of the
poor or the aristocratic

We, as kids, used to engage in a spying game
Knowing which family that had finished cooking
through advance-spying was the aim
There was a culture of serving children who came
Each of us would have at least rice and a piece of
meat to claim

None of us would demand any seat
We were contented sitting on the ground to eat

In many households we in fact ate with glee
We were hardly satiated, as we would move to the
neighbouring house for another spree

There was Christmas rice in every kitchen
We would be served it with beef or chicken
It would normally be brought in a tray
Sometimes we would be in a hurry to eat and failed
to pray

IGNORANCE KILLED TALENTS BUT NOT NOW

All parents meant well for their children
However, being in ignorance decades ago, they did not allow their wards to reign
This killed so many talents
They were stifled by lack of advancements

The emphasis of many parents was on education
So much skills and talents suffered abnegation
Many precocious youths gave up such skills
There was no opportunity to engage in appropriate drills

The awareness of earnings abroad was low
This was the situation until about four decades ago
Before then, for playing football, a child would be denied food
Attending a musical show was interpreted as an act of a disoriented childhood

Concerts as just humorous plays were allowed
However, an aspiration to become an actor was disallowed
Some kids passionate on their ambitions ran away
Their success has created more awareness today

Successful footballers, musicians and actors have changed the situation
Parents now pressure their children into emulation
There is no more spanking

There is no more flogging

In place of denial of food, more is given
Any student who uses his study time for practice is easily forgiven
There is no more total skills-abhorence
There is a virtual acquiescence

Football, music and acting are now major attractions
Parents encourage their gifted children to be part of the actions
Who will not want to benefit from fame and mega bucks?
Who will not be happy receiving money in trucks?

THE FOOTBALL OWNER AS A COACH AND A REFEREE

It was rare for parents to buy football for a son
So many discouraging reasons were given under the sun
This was in our adolescent years
It had to do with their fears

They feared the boy would lose direction
They wanted full concentration on studies or education
Rarely, parents would buy their son a ball
Who played would be who the boy called

He also would choose who played on which side
What amounted to a foul play was for him to decide
He could suddenly clutch the ball and threaten to leave
All would then plead with him to forgive

Do not mark him well
If you did, his ego would swell
It would be perceived as rough tackle
That would be the end of the football battle

THE EXTINCT MAGICIANS

They were very visible until some years ago
One would likely see them by major markets in their
promo
A magician would spread a mat or two on the ground
He put down his paraphernalia and would start
dancing around

The major things would be a long wooden box
It would be covered with a colour of the blood of an
ox
There would be some idols or fetish objects
There might be a bell and other gadgets

A crowd would gather after a short while
He would ask them to chorus a refrain as he engaged
in his wile
A magician had shown envelopes stuffed with papers
to the spectators
He then asked those interested in having them to give
money as donors

The papers in the envelope were of currency sizes
The impression was that the donors would reap heavy
prizes
He continued his incantations of voodoo
He made gesticulations with juju

"When I say appear, you say appear"
The crowd would chorus "appear"
He dipped his hands into the clothe-covered box

Unknown to them, the whole thing was a hoax

The 'empty' box he showed them earlier had a false
bottom
There he hid other envelopes in the bosom
He then brought them out
He gave them to the donors as handout

When each opened his, he saw a copper ring
None of them wanted such a thing
They thought they would receive notes of currency
They kept what he gave them with hesitancy

He said the ring was antidote to all accidents
How would a dead victim react to such incidents?
Some of them requested a refund
He refused, and they were stunned

A DOOR TO NOWHERE

One is in my community
Some in western Nigeria, of no close proximity
It is a one-storey structure
Of traditional architecture

A door upstairs leads nowhere
It is not as if there is a veranda there
Anyone venturing beyond the door crashes outside
It will be like attempting suicide

One keeps imagining the intention behind putting that
door
Could it be that it is just for décor?
It is such a monumental risk
Windows would have sufficed if the aim was to
ensure escape from danger in a manner brisk

Nevertheless, each building shows creativity
Our forebears deserve applause for their ingenuity
Some of these houses have been there for decades
This is even when there have not been upgrades

The walls are made of mud fortified with palm wood
The decking is made of hardwood
Windows and doors were constructed with planks
Some of the planks in the deck are held together with
yanks

Such buildings in the days of our forebears were only
for the opulent

The fact that they dwarf others shows they were built
by the affluent
However, anybody approaching that door has to be
aware
It is intriguing that a door upstairs leads nowhere

THE FOUR-YEARLY VISITOR

He is our town's man
We are not particularly his fan
This is because we see him only every four years
When elections are imminent he appears

He comes to distribute rice and salt in small quantities
The types he shares are even those of low qualities
Yes, he is our kinsman
He is a well-known political helmsman

He is a legislator
He is a member of the National Legislature
He has been there for two decades
He moves with motorcades

Regarding facilities in our communities, there is an acute dearth
Twenty years ago he promised us heaven on earth
We have not seen heaven
But he has built for himself a magnificent haven

We appreciate his constituency project of a pit toilet
Compare it to his personal billion-naira mall up 'to let'
We are now determined to let another person go
This will certainly bruise our four-yearly visitor's ego

THE AUGUST MEETING

The women are all home
They are set for their yearly welcome
This is their meeting in August
It is treated by them as very august

They attend the gathering in their gaily uniform
There are no sorts of variform
Their headgears are elegantly tied
Blouses are worn in a manner that make them dignified

God bless our women
They have made happier we men
They are virtually jettisoning Hollandais for the season
Their preference now to the far cheaper wax is the reason

Their meeting is always of great interest
No woman in Igboland shows disinterest
The essence is the progress of each town
They foot the bills on their own

They complement men's effort
This gives us a lot of comfort
They chart the path of peace and development
They, in the process, assist in meeting the communities' requirement

It is often a solemn gathering

It is devoid of bickering
No one has guts to disgust the gusts of the august
August assembly
We salute our women for carrying on avowedly

TOUCH NOT YOUR PALM FRUITS

The town has banned the harvesting of palm fruits
until Yule-month
Thereafter, there will be a communal harvesting and
sale for one month
The proceeds will be used for community
development
The earlier generations ensured community education
empowerment.

The Catholic or Anglican Church was the common
denomination
We now witness more Christian divagation
Communal efforts for one church's growth is no more
tenable in diversity
However, when it comes to general development,
there is unity

The bonafide owners resume ownership after the
communal harvesting
They will still recoup whatever they are investing
It is a win-win situation
Communities gain from such a developmental
acceleration

Bunches of palm fruits are sold in a heap
The buyers, mainly women, still have profits to reap
A form of auction process is involved
The highest bidder is favoured

THE CLAY SAFE

I had yearly, in my adolescence, a safe
Our parents encouraged us to save
It was made of clay
Its colour was gray

It was a piggybank but moulded round
Being delicate, it was always placed on the ground
The small opening in it was slant
It was designed so that money could not be removed
even if one was in want

Some people gave children money during festivities
We benefitted periodically from such activities
We were, of course, bound to inform our parents
We were, in fact, not known to conceal presents

Whenever we were given money, we saved it
Even if we were hungry we would not buy anything to
eat
We were happy increasing our savings
The competition to save more fuelled my cravings

We therefore imbibed a saving habit
The safe was like a bank into which one made deposit
At the end of each year, the safes were broken
Accounts of all the contents would then be taken

The highest saver, among the children, would be
rewarded

A new pair of shoes or clothes or some other thing
would be awarded
The past savings were then left in the custody of our
parents
They were used as part of the money in building our
own house, instead of paying rent

MILLIONS ON THE DEAD

The craze is increasing by the day
The bereaved go out of their way
They, in the urge to impress, spend millions of naira on the dead
It has become a competition and the quest of who will take the lead

The corpse is deposited in the morgue for long
Very elaborate preparations commence along
A committee is set up
Eminent persons are part of the setup

Sub-committees take up different roles
There must not be loopholes
Massive building renovations commence
It can also be new houses and the fence

Giant billboards are raised
These announce the departure of the deceased
Superlative descriptions of the deceased are common
Publicity in the television and radio goes on

Assorted carnival-like uniforms are sewn
Enormous wood for cooking will be hewn
The D-day is here
The whole nation will hear

The ceremony will be heralded with hundred Canon shots
The occasion will be attended by all the big shots

Thousands have to pay their last respect
Given the deceased's status, it is what we all expect

Funeral service will be officiated by a big clergy
It takes place in a very big arena, for synergy
Sermon and orations will depict the deceased is already in heaven
He will be described as a professionally thorough-bred maven

The burial is followed by a grand reception
High-pitched sounds vibrate from different directions
Musical bands play in vantages
It is as if there is music for all races

Lavish burials are not common with every faith
There is wisdom in the modesty of those who fete less as they surrender to fate
Moslem burials do not involve too much cash
After all, the Holy Books say we come from and will return to ash

FRIDAY EVENING REVELRY

Shortly the sun will set
The bar attendants are ensuring the tables are preset
Prospective patrons are also leaving their work or business
They are anxious to savour the evening's goodness

It is a roadside spot, on a Friday
There will be no work the next day
The drinkers leave very late
An opportunity to forget their worries as they profligate

The tables are filled with bottles and drinking glasses
The music renting the air is for all classes
Black and green bottles compete
This circle of friends are complete

One man was mischievous
He was repassing, after two hours, in manner surreptitious
He murmured something with subdued assertiveness
It turned out he said that the drinkers were sustaining the breweries in business

Did he want the breweries to shut down?
Would that earn him a crown?
Another passer-by screened in impatience
"I hope these men will not become hospital patients"

The advertisements urge responsible drinking

This presupposes proper thinking
A person can drink out his soul
It means he has no more important goal

Those who harken to the brewers' advice drink
responsibly
This can still make the breweries operate profitably
The problem is more with the drunk
He may end up as a junk

THE RAIN MAKERS

A celebrant in the rainy season wants a clear sky
He desires that the day be very dry
He then involves a rainmaker
Isn't this an obvious misnomer?

Those in the art and act play dual roles without pain
They can draw down or prevent rain
Some rainmakers start their work few days before an occasion
They ostensibly reduce the cloud density to prevent much accumulation

If rain does not fall, there will be a smooth occasion
They will, of course, wallow in adulation
If incidentally it falls, they will attribute it to a rival
The rival supposedly drew down the rain in betrayal

Some celebrants therefore engage all the rainmakers in the vicinity
These include those in the locality and the entire community
There will be many of them waving brooms all about
On some occasions, they are defied as it rains throughout

Some rainmakers do not just wave any broom
They ignite certain woods whose smoke supposedly disperse the clouds and their gloom
They then look up to the sky muttering the esoteric

This appears to be the language with which they
communicate to the atmospheric

Some rainmakers have their mystical ground stone
They place their rain matchetes on this to hone
Rainmakers have their worth at every festival
Their impact is there, even if it is merely psychological

A RAINY DAY

I raced home as the clouds thickened
The sky was rumbling and children were frightened
It was in the afternoon
My car radio was playing a tone and I could not but croon

I arrived home just at the nick of time
I had prayed for the small fuel in the car to take me home as I had no more dime
I spent all I had at the market
I discovered that there was nothing again in my pocket

The rain came in torrents
There were no dull moments
It was raining cats and dog
My family started praying to God

We actually lived by a slope
We got ready a long rope
Should there be flood, we would throw it over and climb a tree
This would make us danger-free

There were staccato sounds on our zinc roof
They were not music to hoof
The rain however started to recede, to our relief
God really answered our prayers, in our belief

The uncompleted drainage system has survived three Administrations
The present one seems to be hearing our protestations
The workers are back to site this time
It is evident that they are working overtime

WELCOMING SNAILS AS THEY BREAK FROM HIBERNATION

This is dry season
Snails have been out of their shells preseason
They have now gone into hibernation
It is always something of a consternation

They are on self-imprisonment
They rely on food for their aliment
This is among their wonderful features
It is not common with other creatures

Many go into the soil
Searching for them on land surface becomes a fruitless toil
Digging them out involves a lot of travail
The labour can also be to no avail

They break out at the dawn of the rainy season
This time, rain can fall for some hours without ceasing
The shelled gastropod will break their membrane
They will start crawling out no matter the terrain

These animals creep out at night
To find them, one would need light
They assemble more in ground foliage
To harvest a good quantity one has to forage

THE VILLAGE POND

This is our nearest source of water
It is a collection of flowing rainwater
It is located at the far end of the village square
It is shallow at the entrance but deeper further

The wall and floor are natural earth
Without it, in the dry season, we will have water
dearth
The rains result to its brimming
It is however neither for drinking nor cooking

It is for certain domestic chores
These include washing of dishes, pots and clothes
It is also used for processing palm fruit
It is equally employed for the extraction of breadfruit

Usage of its water is prohibited in the rainy season
This is because it is a reservoir for post rainy season
The pond is dredged before it starts raining
This is for the purpose of clearing mud and ensuring
more water holding

THE IROKO

The Iroko is the king of our tropical forest
It towers above the rest
Its roots stretch to several feet
The tap root can be tens of metres deep

Its trunk is so gigantic
It can only be partly gripped by hands proverbially magnetic
The climber risks tripping
There is always the likelihood of his slipping

One cannot therefore climb it the conventional way
This is if one truly wants to see another day
So a rope is hauled across a stem
It is then joined with the other end of the item

Our forefathers never felled an Iroko without sacrifice
Incantations alone would not suffice
For us now that was fetishism
We consider such an act of paganism

Climbing it involves holding the rope on two sides
Then one will be marching the Iroko as one upwardly glides
An Iroko cannot be felled as a whole
The climber will first cut the branches to sizes of a bole

It is unreasonable to fell an Iroko without trimming

This is because such an action can be dangerous and
harming
It will jeopardize the safety of persons and buildings
around
The deafening sound of a falling Iroko always makes
people astound

I LOVED THE NIGER DELTA

It used to be exciting to behold the Niger Delta
This lush green area had a very positive data
The place was full of aquatic splendour
It had all the trappings of a grandeur

It was so rich a vegetation
Then the region had not witnessed oil exploration
The water was so pure and real
The atmosphere had a calming appeal

What a fresh and solemn air!!!
What a human habitation, with a lair!!!
What amazing plants and mammals!!!
What a constant joy of nature in our annals!!!

The land paid the sea compliment
A wonderful good neighbourliness it was, in complement
Palm trees competed with bamboos for height
They soared to catch the soothing sunlight

I so much loved my Niger Delta
Give me back a Niger Delta without hydra
It will be my place in re-incarnation
What it will be then is in my imagination

OIL IS STRUCK

Mother fortune smiled on us when oil was struck
We had minded our fishing and farming until this luck
The explorers had previously and unsuccessfully worked and toiled
It was as if all their efforts were foiled

Oloibiri became the goose that would first lay the golden egg
There was no fear of it being stolen by any yegg
None worried about any killjoy
Envisaged was an Eldorado of re-enjoy

The journey of the petro-dollar had started
Though what it fully held in stock was uncharted
The rigs were the drilling tools of subterranean adventure
They were the nose-diving instruments of peradventure

Before then, they could eke out nothing
Then they hit oil at a sleuthing
It was in commercial quantity
Furthermore, this was a crude of high quality

The exploration in other places was fruitless
Were the gods angry or powerless?
Did Oloibiri offer sacrifices in propitiation?
Could it be hers was more in proportion?

TAKE ME TO THE GARDEN CITY

By the south-eastern shores of Nigeria is a place
The Atlantic Ocean stares it on the face
It is by the Bight of Benin
It was virtually free from vermin

There indeed was a Garden City
It was a peaceful, industrial and commercial entity
Port Harcourt was the cleanest city in Nigeria
The town-planning and flowers gave no room for claustrophobia

It was a beehive of economic activities
The skilled and unskilled worked with vivacity in full capacities
Port workers busied as crude oil was exported
Commerce thrived and industries were supported

Bank credits and employment knew no bound
Workers and traders had money to throw around
Everything about it was aesthetic
Man harnessed the work of God in a manner very fantastic

Beautiful flowers adorned its landscape
Folks from stressful towns trooped in, on weekends, in escape
Joe Nez, however, sang he was there for a treasure
He said he was not there for pleasure

I remember the Garden City with nostalgia

It is indeed a great feeling of euphoria
Take me to the Garden City!!!
What a place so pretty!!!

THE TATTOOED GREEN

Black and blood are the Niger Delta's new colours
Oil exploration has consumed the virgin mangrove contours
Green vegetation has assumed an opaque foliage
Where then can we forage?

No hope exists for the aquatic
Unregulated oil exploration is chaotic
The fishermen thus further away wander
The search for fish is now more elusive even in a trawler

The seafood lovers may wait in vain
Hunger for such will surely cause them further pain
Their plates will not, unlike before, witness fish
They will have to eat another dish

One is on water, by water, on one's brink
Yet there is none to drink
Oil sludge slugs heavily on aquatic life
One can cut the sedimentation with a knife

Gas from flares exacerbate the ecosystem
Man, animals and plants witness an endangered system
Farms are terribly famished
Animals, mammals and fish are finitely finished

Our greenery has been brazenly tattooed
The explorers should be tabooed

Who will bell the cat?
Bring in the Niger Delta super-brat

TRAPPED IN OUR FORTUNE

Cry, dear compatriots
Let us draw the government's attention, patriots
The goose that lays the golden egg is dying
Our sea, rivers and creeks are crying

Bioterrorism is on the offensive
We cannot continue to remain passive
The oil in the region should increase our purse
It should not in any way be a curse

Water creatures are now awash with blood
Our cities' landscape often re-floods
The environment is awash with pollution
Oil spill is worsening the condition

Some claim there is genocide
Why are we also slaughtering ourselves in fratricide?
Is it all because of oil and politics?
Should we not have stopped at polemics?

Some places are witnessing frequent sporadic
shooting
Let a chance be given to troubleshooting
There are areas where bombs and bullets rain
Terror should not continue to reign

We are obviously trapped in our fortune
Our oil has become a misfortune
Cults, armed gangs, kidnappers, illegal bunkers are
putting the region in self-immolation

Multi nationals and local collaborators are fuelling our annihilation

Blood is thicker than oil
Don't set me against my brother in turmoil
No one should make our resource a war spoil
Fear God, respect the law, don't despoil

GENERALS EVERYWHERE

There are generals
There are also generals
Many were born in the wake of agitation
This was when our region gravitated towards
fragmentation

Generals we knew were in their garrisons and
battalions
They only left there for operations
Their enlistments, training and postings were in public
domain
Their faces and public activities are in multidomain

The accoutrements of known generals are original
Their appearance and outfits are regimental
Their arms are from approved armoury
They are not from any source that is unsavoury

The generals we know are gazetted
None is ever known to be undocumented
These are our generals
There are, however, now some undesirables

These other generals are in the estuaries, creeks and
forest
The generals we know are after them so they do not
rest
We do not know when the undesirables had got ranks
There was no rank decoration and celebration with
bands

Their headquarters are neither Division, Garrison nor
Battalion Headquarters
They are ensconced in their camps in strange
quarters
Each self-styled general controls his own enclave
There he and his gang hold their conclave

Both sets of generals meet sometimes
This is at battle-raging times
We have generals everywhere, some genuine, others
ragtags
The ragtags survive on monetary contents of piracy
and kidnapping ransom bags

We need our Generals
We do not want anymore the ephemerals
But let the powers that be hear the cry of the region
and the people
Let them do the needful and avoid goose pimple

WHERE ARE THE WEAPONS FROM?

There is a proliferation of illegal arms
The joker will say they were given to insurgents and militants as alms
Is it conceivable to give alms of sophisticated weapons?
Who gives criminals military camouflage crepon?

Some think they are not gotten from our soil
They feel it is from unscrupulous merchants who exchange them for money or blood oil
Others claim they are taken from the nation's agents
They are not specific as to the affected contingents

Where are they hidden?
Is the disclosure by anyone forbidden?
We thought they were surrendered during the amnesty
Now we know there was no hundred percent honesty

They claim they do not trust the other party
The other party has always expressed sincerity
The people still suffer militancy
There are damages even with our military supremacy

Our gallant troops have defeated the insurgents
They recovered large armaments
The defeat is however technical
The insurgents resurface in maneuvers that are tactical

A northern nation is in hostility
Her renegade fighters are reinforcing the insurgents'
capability
Each renegade brings additional arm
This is causing us so much harm

THE FATHERS AND THE YOUTHS

The fathers are behind the scene
All the activities in the region they have seen
They attribute them to the boys
The national economy suffers boils

Some call the acts 'agitation'
Others see it as confrontation
The boys seem to enjoy the fathers' blessing
The fathers appear to be doing some window-
dressing

The central government knows the fathers
She can only get to the boys through their radars
The fathers know the boys' grievance
These coincide with the region's annoyance

The fathers protect the youths, as demanded by all
cultures
They also do not want to be seen as vultures
Between the men and government it is a cat-and-
mouse game
Between the men and the boys it is the same

The demands are too many
The government finds some uncanny
The authorities have listening ears or so they say
They ask for patience day-by-day

The youths are impatient and frenzy
Some actions by them are crazy

An example is their blowing up oil pipelines
They are also planting explosives and mines

Some expatriates are leaving because of kidnapping
They do not want to be caught napping
The authorities have done a lot in good faith
The youths wonder if that could have been the case
had they resigned to fate

OUR MANGROOVE HOUSE

Deep in the rainforest lies our abode
It is perched on stems with underwater overstrode
Here we are at home with nature
We share our environment with any adaptive creature

It has been the place of our ancestors
We have not been displaced by rampaging investors
Here we wither weather's vagaries
We live without much rumblegaries

Wood, leaves, raffia or palm ropes are the material
They are all gotten from our alluvial
The construction is done by our direct labour
We also had the assistance of our neighbour

The walls are of planks
There are wooden bridges to houses at some flanks
You can paddle and park your canoe by your hut
You must have space to sail through without hurt

There, we put all our worldly possessions
We do not suffer any obsessions
We are contented with our little world
What we eat and drink is in our ward

ANY JOURNEY IN THE WOODEN BOAT

Two paddlers man the wooden boat
Their job is to keep it afloat
It is a cheap means of water transport
It is close to travelers and does not need a seaport

The canoeists can anchor the wooden contraption by
any river bank
Many of the boats have seen years as evidenced from
their body plank
The nails are now rusty brownish brands
The planks were nailed and held with flat metallic
bands

Passengers seat on any available crosspiece
Usually in calm water, their minds are at peace
The crosspieces provide additional strength to the
canoe as it glides
The paddlers know the routes and try to avoid the
sea tides

There is enough room for a ton of goods and some
passengers
There is a paddler at each end, both of whom are
divers
They obey the sea waves
And paddle carefully to avoid digging passengers'
graves

Some passengers can, however, be so fearful
Non-swimmers become particularly tearful

Such people during the journey do not feel alright
They become relaxed only when they alight

The brave and the swimmers, whether there is
turbulence or not, care less
They can be said to be careless
The canoeists also always betray no emotion
It does not bother, whether the canoe is in smooth or
rough motion

www.ingramcontent.com/pod-product-compliance
Lightning Source LLC
Chambersburg PA
CBHW051731040426
42447CB00008B/1080